Friction

By the end of this book you will know more about:
- The force called friction.
- Where friction happens.
- How to increase and reduce friction.

You will:
- Plan and carry out fair test investigations.
- Make and test predictions.
- Use graphs and charts to present information.

⭐ **Forces are pushes or pulls that make things move, stop, change direction or change shape.**

Task 1 — Forces concept map

✸ Use these words to make a forces concept map like the one opposite.

push   pull   magnets   gravity   pole   force   south   change   north   direction

✸ Write the words on paper, cut them out and glue them onto a large piece of card.

✸ Join the words together with arrows.

✸ Write on the lines between each word to show how they are linked.

✸ Look at this picture. How many forces are in action? Make a list.

Use a Newton meter to measure pull forces.

Measuring a pull force

You can measure a pull force using a Newton meter (sometimes called a forcemeter).
You should have some Newton meters in your school. They are used to find out how much pull force it takes to make something move.
Forces are measured in 'Newtons'.

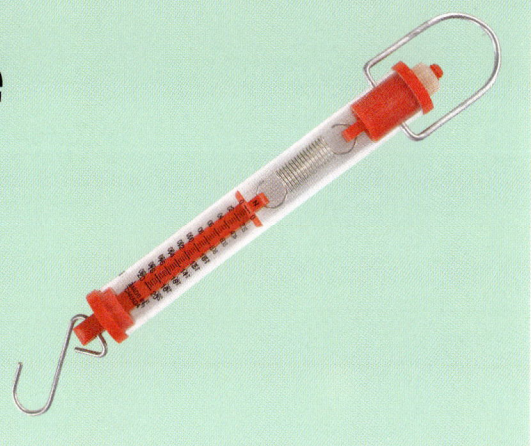

Task 2 — Different Newton meters

- What is different about each of the Newton meters in the picture?

- Why do you think you need different kinds of Newton meters?

- What would you use the first Newton meter for?

- What would you use the last one for?

- Try out different Newton meters around the classroom. Write down what happens.

- Write down the measurements on the different Newton meters on Task Sheet 1.

- Complete the table on Task Sheet 2.

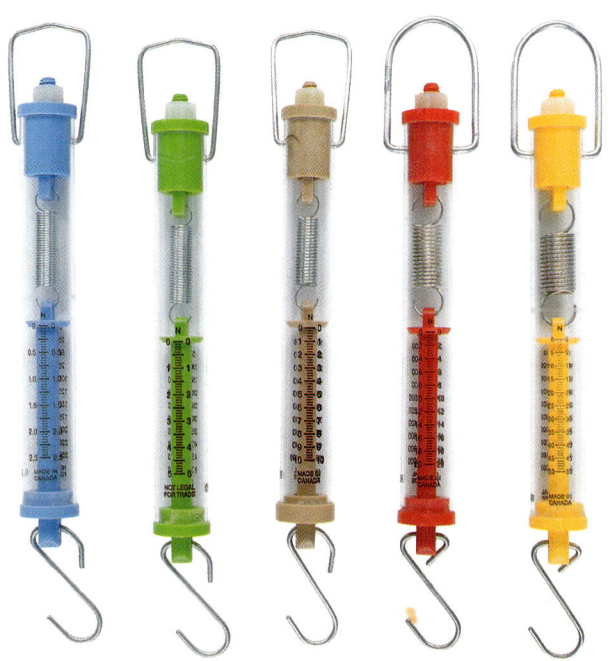

⭐ **Objects move more easily over some surfaces than others.**

Task 3 *Feeling surfaces*

💥 Feel each surface.

💥 Write down 3 words to describe each surface.

YOU NEED:
- piece of carpet
- sheet of glasspaper
- vinyl floor tile
- block of wood

💥 Over which surface do you think it would be easiest to move an object?

💥 Why did you make your choice?

💥 Write down your ideas.

4

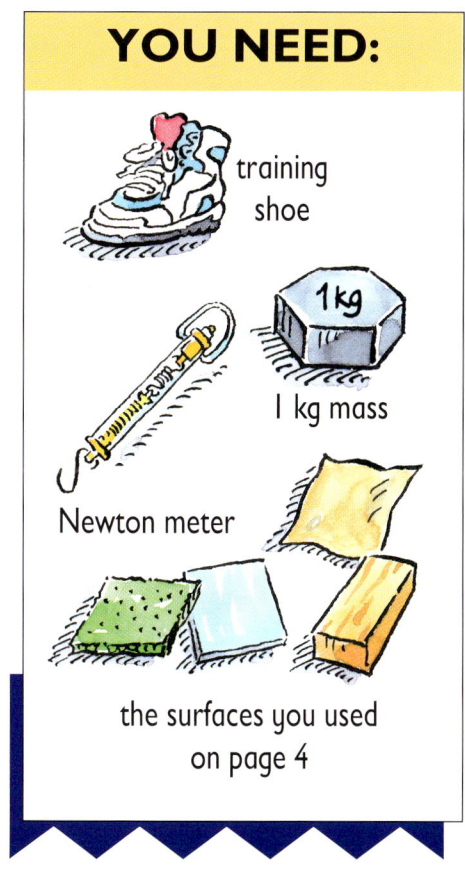

YOU NEED:

- training shoe
- 1 kg mass
- Newton meter
- the surfaces you used on page 4

Task 4 *Getting moving*

- Put the 1 kg mass in the trainer.

- Use the Newton meter to measure the pull force it takes to **start** the trainer moving.

Sometimes it is hard to read the Newton meter and to know exactly how much pull force it took to start something moving.

For this reason, we take several readings so that we can be sure that our answer is about right.

- Take 3 readings for each surface. Record your readings on a table like this:

- Find the middle one of the 3 readings and put it in the last column.

- Now list the surfaces in order of how much force it takes to get the trainer moving.

Put the surface that needs the least force at the top of the list and the surface that needs the most force at the bottom.

⭐ **Make and test predictions.**
Plan and carry out a fair test.

Task 5 — **Scientific Enquiry**
Slopes and surfaces

3,4

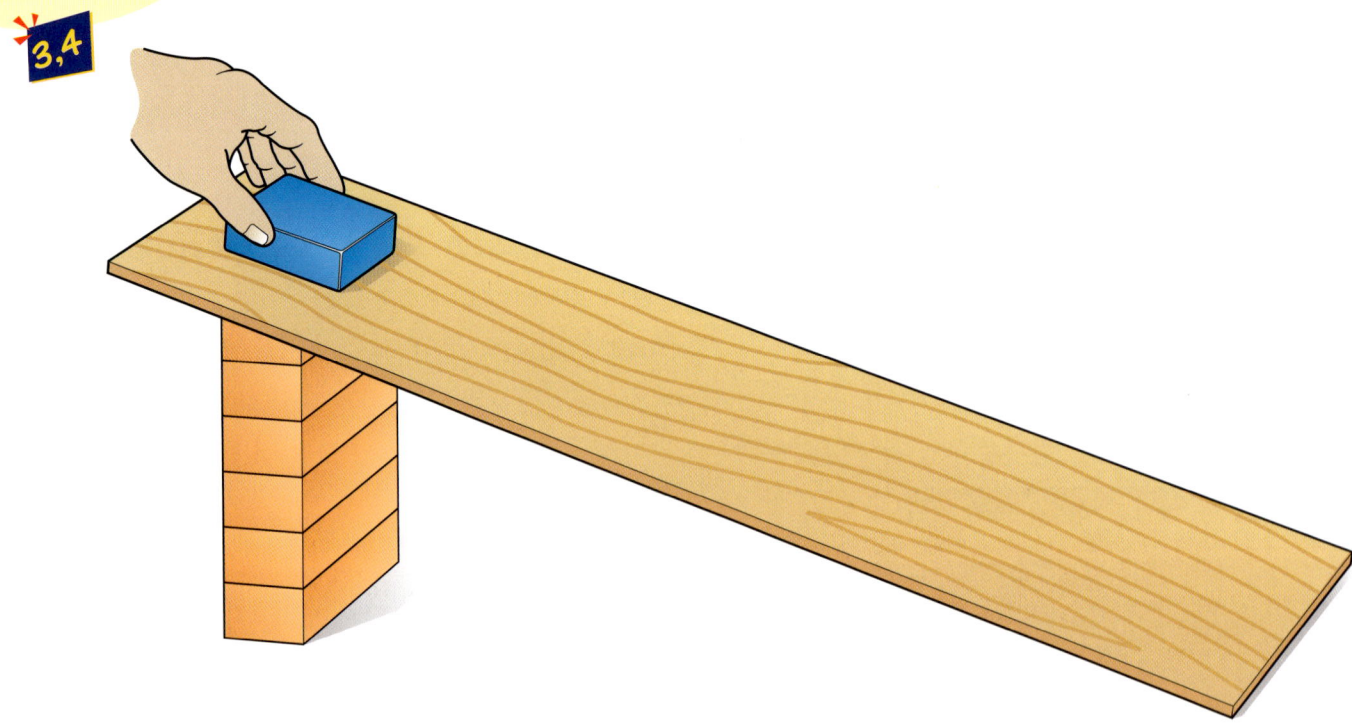

🌟 Look at the picture above.

🌟 How will the height of the pile of bricks affect whether the wooden block moves down the wooden plank?

🌟 Write down your prediction using this opener:
"I think that the more bricks the ..."

6

- Plan and carry out a fair test investigation to find out if your prediction was correct.
- Use Task Sheet 3 to help you.
- When you have finished, use your results to complete the table on Task Sheet 3.

Number of bricks	Did the block move?
0	
1	

- Write down what you found out from your investigation. Use this opener: *"I found out that ..."*
- Which is the best height for the plank to make the wooden block start to move?
- Repeat your investigation using Task Sheet 4, but this time find out if the type of surface covering the plank affects when the wooden block starts to move.

- Draw a graph of your results.
- When you have finished, write down your conclusions.

The _____ was the best surface because...

⭐ **Friction is a force between surfaces in contact.**

Friction

Friction happens when one surface moves over another.

When one surface moves easily over another, there is low friction.

When one surface moves with difficulty over another, there is high friction.

High friction slows things down.

Task 6 — High and low friction

✦ The objects are made of different materials, some smooth and some rough.

✦ Try moving the objects over each other.
How easy is it to move them?

✦ Which objects have high friction when they move over each other? Which have low friction?

✦ Record your answers like this:

shiny paper + silky fabric =
brick + glasspaper =

✦ Try 8 other combinations and record the results.

YOU NEED:

2 pieces of shiny paper

2 pieces of silky fabric

2 plastic lemonade bottles

2 bricks

2 sheets of glasspaper

8

Task 7 *Making friction*

- Take two hairbrushes and move one over the surface of other.
- What happens?
- Where are the push forces in action?
- Write down your ideas.

YOU NEED:

2 hairbrushes

Did you notice how the bristles of the brushes bent?

This is because they are pushing back against your push, making it harder to move them smoothly across each other.

Words to learn and use:
contact
force
friction
move
rough
slow
smooth
surface

9

Task 8 Using friction

⭐ Here are some pictures of friction in action.

Car tyre

Shoelace

Goalkeeper's glove

Ice skate

⭐ How can high friction be useful to us?

⭐ How can low friction be useful to us?

⭐ Write down your ideas.

⭐ How does each of the things shown here create high or low friction?

Extra Challenge

- Explain what friction forces are in action in the picture above.

- Why can a rainy day be dangerous inside a school?

- What could you do to change low friction into high friction in the picture above?

- Write down some ideas, using what you already know about friction.

- How would your changes make the school a safer place in wet weather?

Rainy day at school

There are ways of reducing and increasing friction.

Task 9

Scientific Enquiry
Reducing friction

The children of Class 6 were investigating this question:

What is the best way to reduce friction?

 Their challenge was to get the brick to the other side of the tray with the least amount of pull force.

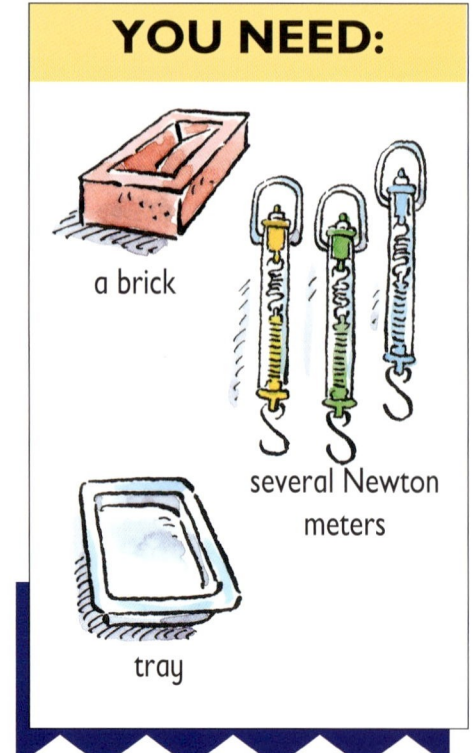

YOU NEED:
a brick
several Newton meters
tray

 Plan and carry out a fair test investigation to answer the question for Class 6.

 Use Task Sheet 5 to help you.

 What could you put on the tray to reduce friction?

 When you have finished, write a set of instructions for Class 6 so that they can also carry out your investigation.

 At each stage of your instructions, explain what forces are in action and how you are reducing friction.

YOU NEED:

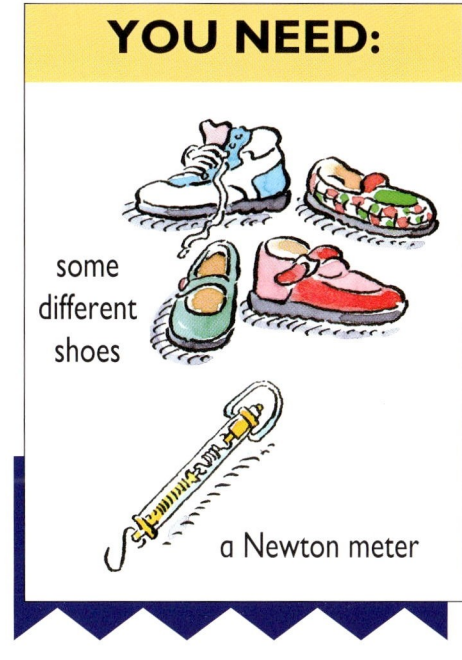

some different shoes

a Newton meter

Scientific Enquiry

Task 10 *Which shoe is best?*

On a slippery floor you do not want to reduce friction but increase it.

- Collect four different shoes from your teacher.

- Which shoe would be best for wearing on a slippery floor?

- Write down the reason for your answer.

Trainers

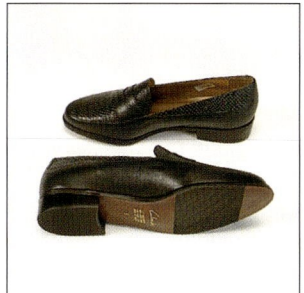
Ordinary shoes

Wellington boots

Slippers

- Plan and carry out a fair test investigation to find out if your prediction was correct.

  Use Task Sheet 6 to help you.

- What kind of graph or chart will you draw to display your results?

- Which shoe was the best on a slippery floor?

- Why? Write down your answer.

- Why do we wear different shoes for different activities?

13

Water resistance is a friction force that slows down objects moving through water.

Water resistance

Friction does not only occur between solid surfaces.

Friction between water and the surface of a moving object is called water resistance.

Water resistance can make movement through water difficult.

Task 11 *Feel the resistance*

- Have you ever tried to walk from one side of a swimming pool to the other through the water?
- Write down what it felt like.
- Why do you think most fish are shaped like this?

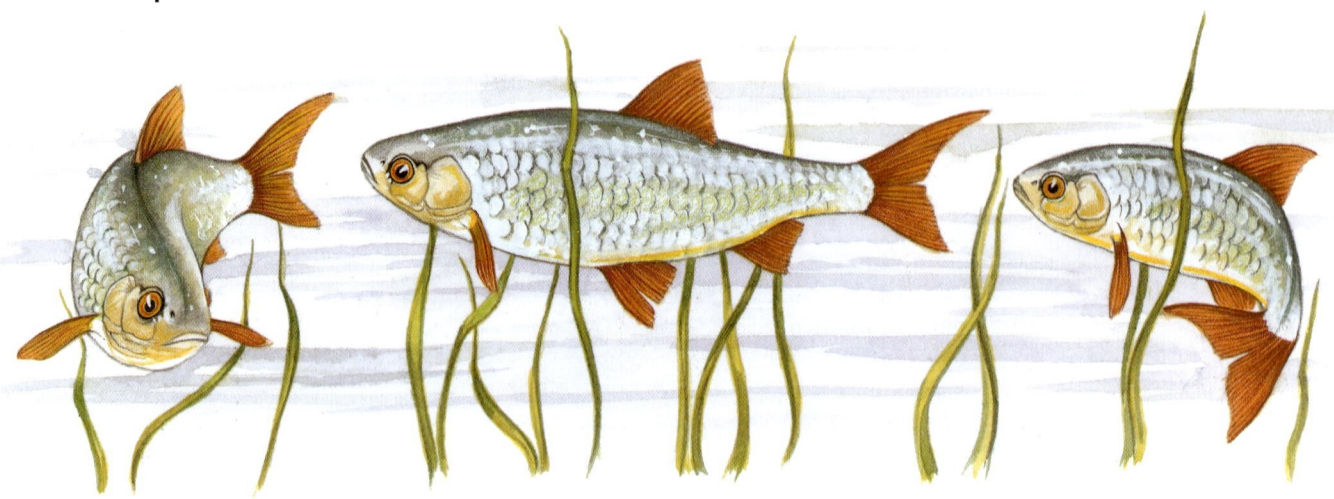

- Why do you think that the boats in the pictures are the shape they are?

Words to learn and use:
increase
reduce
shape
streamlined
water resistance

14

Task 12

Scientific Enquiry

Shapes in water

⭐ Which is the best shape for moving through water quickly?

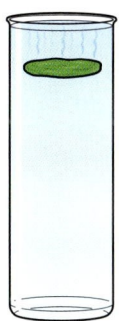  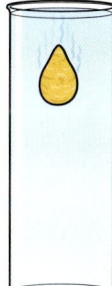 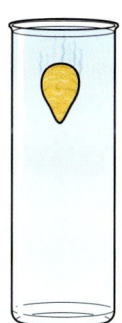

YOU NEED:

Plasticine shapes

tall cylinder full of water or plastic pop bottle with top cut off

⭐ Plan a fair test investigation to answer the question.

⭐ Before you carry out your test, write down which shape you think will be the fastest and why.

⭐ Record your results on a chart like the one below:

⭐ Draw a bar chart using your results.

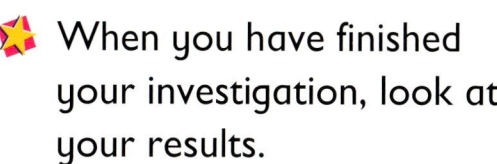

⭐ When you have finished your investigation, look at your results.

⭐ Write a sentence about each shape, explaining what happened and why.

Shapes that cause very little water resistance are said to be **streamlined**.

15

Air resistance is a force that slows down objects moving through air.

Task 13 *Looking at air resistance*

 What do you think is happening in this picture?

YOU NEED:

a piece of paper

 Write a speech bubble explaining your idea.

I think that...

 Hold up a piece of paper and then drop it. Watch what happens.

 Now crumple the paper up.

 Drop it again and watch what happens.

 Why do you think that the crumpled piece of paper fell to the ground more quickly than the flat sheet?

 Write a speech bubble explaining your idea.

Task 14 **Scientific Enquiry**
Parachute puzzler

⭐ Make an investigation to answer this question:

> *How does the size of a parachute affect how long it takes to fall?*

⭐ Use Task Sheet 8.

"How will I make it fair?"

"Will I have to take repeat measurements?"

"How will I record my measurements?"

"What will I measure?"

"What patterns are there in the results?"

⭐ Write in a speech bubble what your results show and explain why.

Make sure you use the words **air resistance** in your speech bubble.

17

Friction is used in everyday life.

1. Handle bar grips
2. Saddle
3. Brakes
4. Tyres
5. Pedal

 **Task 15 Bikes and increasing friction**

- Look at this photograph of a bike.

  Each number is linked to a different part of the bike.

- Write a sentence about each of the numbered parts, explaining how the part increases friction to help the rider of the bike.

- Write your answers in a table.

Bicycle part	Why and how friction is increased
handle bar grips	

Task 16 — Bikes and reducing friction

- Look at this photograph of a racing cyclist.

- What has the rider done to reduce friction so that he can race in the fastest time possible?

- Make a list of your ideas about how friction can be reduced on a bike.

Fact File

Putting friction to work.

Roads on steep hills can be dangerous, because cars and lorries sometimes travel down them too fast.

On some steep hills there are **escape lanes**.

These special lanes at the side of the road are made from a material that slows cars and lorries down so that they can stop safely.

**The Highways Committee
County Hall
Durham**

Class 6
Clairview School
Clairview Road
Durham

25 May 2000

Dear Class 6,

The Highways Committee has decided to create an escape lane on the A146, which has a very steep hill six miles from Durham. As you know, escape lanes are made with special materials that slow lorries and cars down.

The Committee would like you to investigate which materials we should use for this escape lane.

You must provide evidence to support your conclusions.

We look forward to receiving your results.

Yours sincerely,

A Carter
Chair, Highways Committee

Task 17

Scientific Enquiry

Planning an escape lane

 9, 10

- Plan and carry out an investigation to solve the problem for the Highways Committee.

- Use Task Sheet 9 to help you.

- Think about:

- When you carry out the investigation, take careful measurements and record your results.

- When you have finished, write a report for the Highways Committee.

- Think about:

- Now try the task on Task Sheet 10.

Checkpoint

How many forces in action can you spot on this page?

List the forces you can see on Task Sheet 11.

Spot the Forces game

Summary

Which of these do you know and which can you do?

- I know that forces are pushes or pulls that make things move, stop, change direction or change shape.
- I can use a Newton meter to measure pulling forces.
- I know that objects move more easily over some surfaces than others.
- I can make and test predictions.
- I can plan and carry out a fair test.
- I know that friction is a force between surfaces in contact.
- I know how to reduce and increase friction.
- I know that friction is used in everyday life.
- I know that water resistance slows down objects moving through water.
- I know that air resistance slows down objects moving through air.
- I can solve a problem using my knowledge and understanding about friction.

Complete your **Science Log** to show how well you know these and how well you can do them. Circle a face for each statement.

Glossary

air resistance

air resistance - a friction force that slows down aircraft, parachutes and other objects moving through air.

escape lane - a lane at the side of a road that is covered with a special material to slow traffic so that it can stop safely.

force - a push or a pull.

friction - a force between surfaces in contact.

increase - make greater.

Newton meter - an instrument that measures pull forces (sometimes called a forcemeter).

prediction - a statement saying what the result of an event or experiment is likely to be.

reduce - make smaller or less.

surface - the outer edge of an object.

streamlined - specially shaped to reduce air resistance or water resistance.

water resistance - the friction force that slows down boats, animals, swimmers and other objects as they move through water.

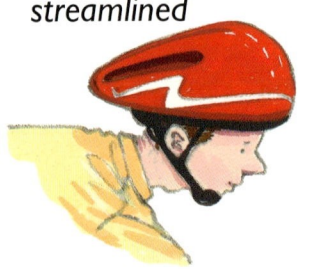
streamlined

water resistance